AMAZING BODY SYSTEMS
CIRCULATORY SYSTEM

by Karen Latchana Kenney

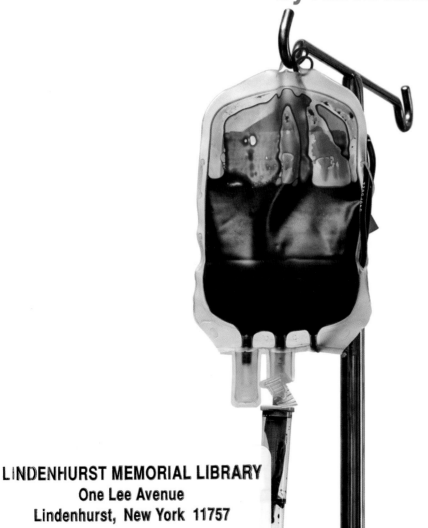

po go

Ideas for Parents and Teachers

Pogo Books let children practice reading informational text while introducing them to nonfiction features such as headings, labels, sidebars, maps, and diagrams, as well as a table of contents, glossary, and index.

Carefully leveled text with a strong photo match offers early fluent readers the support they need to succeed.

Before Reading

- "Walk" through the book and point out the various nonfiction features. Ask the student what purpose each feature serves.

- Look at the glossary together. Read and discuss the words.

Read the Book

- Have the child read the book independently.

- Invite him or her to list questions that arise from reading.

After Reading

- Discuss the child's questions. Talk about how he or she might find answers to those questions.

- Prompt the child to think more. Ask: What other body systems do you know about? What do they do? How might they interact with the circulatory system?

Pogo Books are published by Jump!
5357 Penn Avenue South
Minneapolis, MN 55419
www.jumplibrary.com

Library of Congress Cataloging-in-Publication Data

Names: Kenney, Karen Latchana, author.
Title: Circulatory system / by Karen Latchana Kenney.
Description: Minneapolis, MN: Jump!, Inc. [2017]
Series: Amazing body systems
Audience: Ages 7-10.
Includes bibliographical references and index.
Identifiers: LCCN 2016033549 (print)
LCCN 2016036326 (ebook)
ISBN 9781620315576 (hardcover: alk. paper)
ISBN 9781620315965 (pbk.)
ISBN 9781624965050 (ebook)
Subjects: LCSH: Cardiovascular system—Juvenile literature.
Classification: LCC QP103 .K46 2017 (print)
LCC QP103 (ebook) | DDC 612.1—dc23
LC record available at https://lccn.loc.gov/2016033549

Series Editor: Jenny Fretland VanVoorst
Series Designer: Anna Peterson
Photo Researcher: Anna Peterson

Photo Credits: All photos by Shutterstock except: Getty, 15, 16-17, 20-21; iStock 18-19.

Printed in the United States of America at Corporate Graphics in North Mankato, Minnesota.

TABLE OF CONTENTS

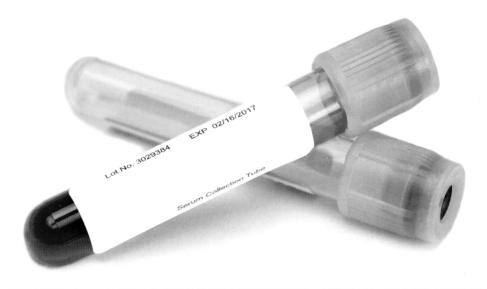

CHAPTER 1

BLOOD HIGHWAY

You run to the park.
You breathe deeply.
Your chest pounds.
Why? That's your heart.
It is working hard.

Check your **pulse**. Do you feel how fast your heart beats? It has to pump **blood** all over your body. It is the main **organ** of the **circulatory system**. This system controls how blood flows and where it goes.

BLOOD FLOW OF THE HEART

OXYGEN-RICH BLOOD

OXYGEN-POOR BLOOD

Blood is the most important fluid in your body. It carries **nutrients** to your cells. It delivers **oxygen**. And it removes **carbon dioxide**, a waste product.

Blood moves through your body in a series of tubes. They are called **blood vessels**. The largest are the **arteries**. They take oxygen-rich blood away from the heart.

Veins carry blood that needs oxygen back to the heart.

The smaller tubes are **capillaries**. Their thin walls let gases through.

TAKE A LOOK!

Your circulatory system is made up of blood vessels. It also includes the heart and lungs.

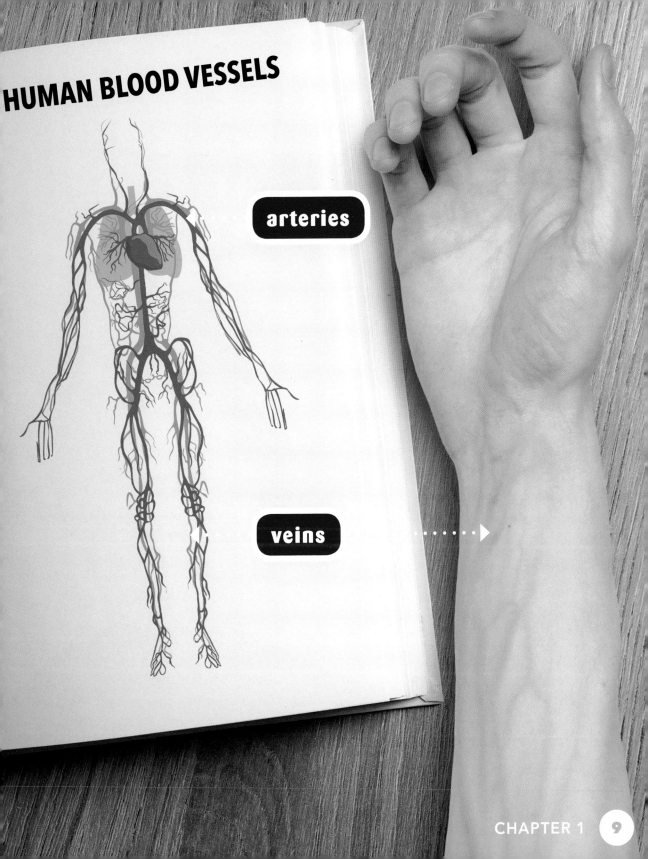

HUMAN BLOOD VESSELS

arteries

veins

CHAPTER 2

THE HEART OF IT ALL

The heart is at the center of this system. It sits in the middle of the chest, between the lungs. It is the size of your fist.

Inside the heart are four chambers. Two are on each side. Blood enters through the upper chambers. **Valves** let blood into the lower chambers. They act as one-way doors. They keep blood moving in the right direction.

The heart is a muscle. It squeezes. It relaxes. It pulls blood in. It pushes blood out.

Even at rest your heart works hard! Just squeeze a tennis ball. It's not easy. That's about the same force your heart uses with every beat.

CHAPTER 3

BEAT BY BEAT

With every beat, your heart pumps oxygen through your body.

With the first beat, it relaxes. The right side fills with blood. The blood needs oxygen. It has to dump carbon dioxide, too. Cells make this gas when they use oxygen.

Then the heart squeezes. That's the second beat.

Blood rushes to the lungs. It picks up oxygen from tiny air sacs called **alveoli**. At the same time, it releases the carbon dioxide it had been carrying. Your lungs dispose of it when you breathe out.

DID YOU KNOW?

The heart beats close to 100,000 times each day. It beats about 3 billion times in an average lifetime.

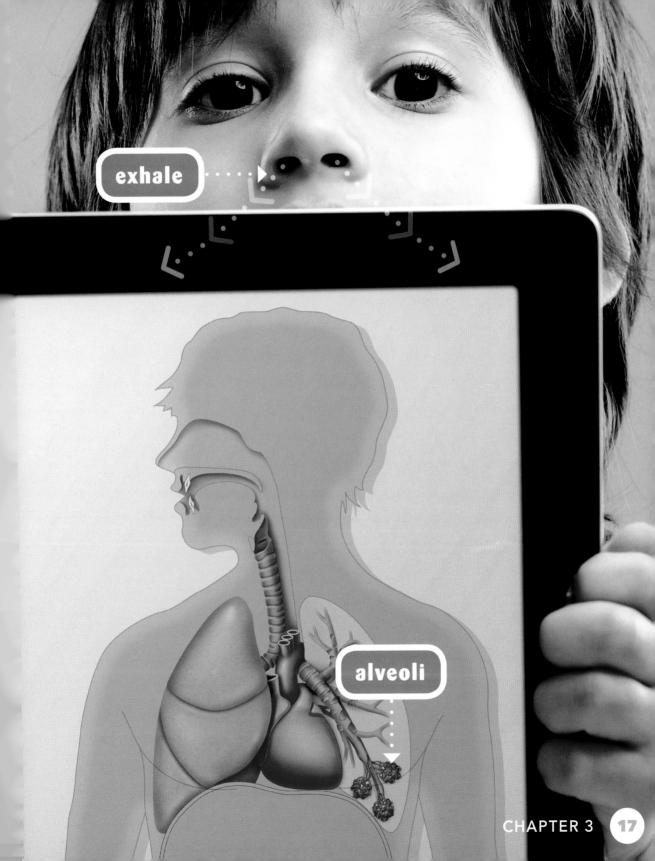

exhale

alveoli

The Human Heart

aorta ···▶

Now the blood flows back to the heart. It enters the left side. It exits through the **aorta**. It is the biggest artery in the body. It branches into smaller arteries. They become capillaries. They reach all parts of the body.

The blood delivers oxygen to all the body's cells. It also picks up new waste.

Now it's time to head back to the heart. The blood flows through veins. It gets pumped into the heart. Then it goes to the lungs again. It collects oxygen. It drops off waste.

So run! Jump! Be active.

Your heart pumps. Your blood flows. Your body gets the oxygen and nutrients it needs.

ACTIVITIES & TOOLS

LISTEN TO THE BEAT

Pair up with a partner and listen to your hearts beating. See how the beats change with exercise.

What You Need:
- a partner
- a cardboard paper towel tube
- a watch

1 Place one end of the cardboard tube in the middle of your partner's chest. Put your ear by the other end. Do you hear your partner's heartbeat?

2 Now count how many beats you hear in 60 seconds. Write the number down.

3 Ask your partner to do jumping jacks for one minute.

4 Listen again to your partner's heartbeat. Count the beats made in 60 seconds. Write the number down.

5 Switch and have your partner listen to your heart beating. Did the beats change after the jumping jacks?

GLOSSARY

alveoli: Tiny air sacs in the lungs.

aorta: The biggest artery in the body.

arteries: Tubes that carry blood away from the heart.

blood: The red fluid that circulates in the heart, arteries, capillaries, and veins of a vertebrate animal; it brings nourishment and oxygen to and carries away waste products from all parts of the body.

blood vessels: Tubes that carry blood throughout the body; they are arteries, capillaries, and veins.

capillaries: Small tubes that carry blood in the body.

carbon dioxide: A colorless, odorless gas that is a byproduct of animal respiration.

circulatory system: The body system that controls blood flow.

nutrients: Substances your body needs to stay healthy and to grow.

organ: A part of the body that does a certain job.

oxygen: A gas found in the air, which people need to live.

pulse: A regular, rhythmic throbbing caused by the squeezing and relaxing of the heart.

valves: Moving parts that control the flow of liquid, such as blood.

veins: Tubes that carry blood to the heart.

INDEX

TO LEARN MORE

Learning more is as easy as 1, 2, 3.

1) Go to www.factsurfer.com

2) Enter "circulatorysystem" into the search box.

3) Click the "Surf" button to see a list of websites.

With factsurfer, finding more information is just a click away.